The Black Rock Desert

Gregory McNamee, SERIES EDITOR

The Black Rock Desert

TEXT BY William L. Fox   PHOTOGRAPHS BY Mark Klett

The University of Arizona Press   Tucson

The University of Arizona Press
© 2002 William L. Fox
First Printing
All rights reserved

♾ This book is printed on acid-free, archival-quality paper.
Manufactured in the United States of America

07   06   05   04   03   02   6   5   4   3   2   1

Library of Congress Cataloging-in-Publication Data appear on the last
printed page of this book.

British Library Cataloguing-in-Publication Data
A catalogue record for this book is available from the British Library.

Frontispiece: Surveying the Black Rock Desert from a volcanic knob

contents

photographs

PHOTOGRAPHS

X

preface

How do a photographer and a writer work together? During the last four years, Mark Klett and I have traveled to dozens of sites in the American West as participants in the ongoing project known as Third View, centered on the concept of re-photographing scenes documented by exploration photographers in the nineteenth century. In the process of our work, we found ourselves increasingly compelled to include new and contemporary sites, while also developing an unusually complementary style of working together.

"Bill, come over here and look at what I'm photographing," Mark might say. "Mark, come over here; maybe you should photograph what I'm looking at," I would offer. At night, while sitting around a campfire or in a motel room while negatives were being washed and dried, we'd talk about what we had seen, and I'd read my field notes out loud.

During each trip a specific theme would emerge early out of the concatenation of images and words. It could be as concrete as regulatory inflation imposed by state and federal agencies seeking to protect endangered viewsheds, or as abstract as how we model time in space in the form of an ascending spiral. The themes, in turn, would help guide both the subsequent photography and writing.

Mark is deeply concerned with our rediscovery of open places, with how we educate ourselves about the natural world and how we fit responsibly within it. In addition to rephotographing the work of artists exploring the West, he has created an extensive body of his own work that presents to us not only the visual facts of these immense spaces but also the interactions of people in and with the landscape. His photography thus creates spatial metaphors as it measures time; it not only pictures the land but also enables us to read how we visually construct landscape as we pass over it.

Mark defines his approach as intuitive; mine is more analytical. The overarching theme for me has been how we convert land into landscape, particularly in deserts, where our perceptual expectations are confounded by spaces that are so large that we have trouble comprehending them.

When Gregory McNamee, the editor of this series, asked me what corner of the desert West I'd be interested in writing about, I replied immediately, "The Black Rock of Nevada." My reasoning was that its immense dry lakebed, the largest playa in North America, is one of the visually most austere places on the planet and thus uniquely suited to defining what a desert is and how we perceive it. When he next asked which photographer I'd like to work with, I likewise had no hesitation. I have had the pleasure of working with several photographers in the West, but it is with Mark that the most synergy for metaphor exists. And that's what it takes to get over cognitive dissonance—the confounding of our perceptual expectations in an isotropic space, where features are uniformly distributed in all directions.

Mark had never been to the Black Rock Desert, and although I have been driving out to it since the late 1960s, I didn't know it as well as necessary to meditate upon it properly. I asked Alvin McLane to orient us for the first couple of days. A legendary field guide and expert on everything from the geology to the archeology of the region, he is also the man I have spent the most time with in the basins and ranges of the American West. It was high time that he and Mark met, and this project was a better excuse than any I could manufacture.

Much of my writing and Mark's photographs document the journeys we take. Although each of us has his poetic moments, often we're more concerned with triangulating our precise position in time and space through rephotography and linear narrative. That isn't the case here. Facts about the Black Rock and an account of the journey are embedded in the text, to be sure, but this book is also about the function of metaphor in space and time, an endeavor more easily discerned through the long sightlines of the desert than in other places.

We offer this collection of collaborative meditations upon a singularity within the American imagination as an encouragement for people to examine how they perceive where they are as they cross the great empty places, rediscovering and recreating the landscape as they go.

The Black Rock Desert

circumference . . .

We get here by following Alvin north out of Reno in our rented minivan and pushing our way through concentric circles of historical aridity. We had a choice of routes when leaving town, either driving north on the Pyramid Highway through the metastasizing suburbs of double-wide manufactured housing and tract homes with their tiny ultra-green lawns, or going east along the Truckee River on Interstate 80 and then turning north through Wadsworth. Either way, we would come to Pyramid Lake, the largest remnant of the giant Pleistocene Lake Lahontan, which once covered much of Nevada.

We chose to follow the river, which flows north out of Lake

Tahoe in the Sierra to pass through Reno and end at Pyramid. It is a typical Great Basin watercourse, in that all the waters of this landlocked physiographic province flow inward to relict lakes or sink into the sediments of the deep basins that sit between the more than three hundred mountain ranges of the region. Tracing the disappearance of a river seemed the right way to start.

Pyramid Lake currently fluctuates at around 370 feet deep, is 27 miles long and 9 miles wide, but is only a fragment of the ancient Lake Lahontan, which at its largest size during pluvial times 50,000 years ago extended over more than 8,665 square miles. You could have rowed a boat from Reno to Idaho during the height of the Pleistocene, which lasted from roughly 2 million until 12,000 years ago.

Skirting the southern end of Pyramid Lake, we passed into another valley that holds Winnemucca Dry Lake, which used to be an intermittent lake during years when Pyramid overflowed. Diversion of the Truckee's waters, however, started in 1903 with the construction of an agricultural canal, which was the first project of the Bureau of Reclamation and continues today with the increasing usage caused by the growth of Reno and the necessity to protect Pyramid's endangered fishes. Pyramid Lake no longer overflows, and now this part of the desert holds water only when storms dump enough rain and snow in the surrounding mountains to create a temporary flood. Its bottom, or playa, holds water half a dozen inches deep for a day, perhaps two, then is dry again. When we drove by at midday, the road bisecting a small lobe of the lakebed, most of the playa was hardened white alkali, but here and there were brownish damp spots caused by runoff from the storms of two weeks earlier.

Cresting a final low saddle spread out over miles to the north, we descended into the watershed of the Black Rock Desert, an enclosed basin that extends up to 80 miles long and 20 miles wide, its elevations between 3,500 and 4,000 feet above sea level. We passed through the hamlet of Empire, which has a modest grocery store that serves the ranchers and farmers scattered around springs and pivot-irrigation plots. Crossing the railroad tracks several miles down the highway, we drove into Gerlach, whose 350 people run five bars and the only gas station within a 10,000-square-mile plot. There's a sign on the far side of town that tells you in no uncertain terms: "Where the pavement ends and the West begins."

To our left Mark and I could see where we were headed, the 400-square-mile playa that is one of the largest unimpeded flat places in North America and the heart of the Black Rock. Frozen in winter, polished by a thin sheet of wind-driven water in the spring, and hot enough to fatally dehydrate humans within hours during the summer, it has been called an "absolute desert," a place where nothing lives permanently atop its surface and where only a few invertebrate species may possibly survive below it.

The Great Basin, that 165,000-square-mile interior drainage of the West that covers most of Nevada and the western half of Utah, was the last province of the United States to be discovered; the Black Rock, which contains one of its thirty-nine major playas into which waters run and none escape, is a recapitulation of the larger region. The playa receives the runoff from 2,600 square miles, an area about two and a half times larger than Rhode Island.

These facts are not unimportant, not here, where they are both dramatic and useful, but they are only a circumference around the body of metaphors necessary for us to describe, or even function in, such an extreme environment. The historical facts, as we know them, begin to accumulate with John C. Frémont, whose 1843–44 expedition members became the first Euro-Americans to see the Black Rock. He called it "a perfect barren" and admitted that "the appearance of the country was so forbidding, that I was afraid to enter it." His language bears witness that he was, if not daring enough to cross it directly, at least able to skirt and describe its edges.

Frémont had a habit, somewhat unusual among his peers in the U.S. Army Corps of Topographical Engineers, of climbing up mountains in order to see not just where he was but also how the land itself was structured. Perhaps it was because he was one of the first American surveyors trained to use an altimeter. He dragged with him a most reluctant German cartographer, Charles Preuss, who, despite his complaints, carefully logged their latitudes and longitudes, the distances traveled and the elevations crossed. Between them they discovered that the Great Basin was an entirely closed hydrographic entity.

Frémont noted that "sterility was the prominent characteristic" of the Great Basin, a system of interior basins that "excites Asiatic, not American ideas." By deploying such rhetoric, the explorer was not only making a valid geographic comparison but also heightening the sense of mystery that still attends to-day to the Great Basin, but most especially to the Black Rock, the kind of place that author Ida Meacham Strobridge, writing at the turn of the twentieth century, would insist should be preserved for "Silence, and Space and the Great Winds."

The map of their journey that Preuss drew helped establish immigrant cutoff trails crossing the Black Rock, leading people later that decade both northwest to Oregon and southwest to the California gold rush. Trying to avoid the fearsome Forty Mile Desert along the more established main trail—a series of playas that so demoralized the immigrants that some are said to have died of existential exhaustion as much as of thirst—they found themselves on a death march equally as harsh, if not more so. In his 1849 journal, artist and chronicler J. Goldsborough Bruff counted 103 dead oxen, 36 horses, and a mule at the last spring before entering the playa and another 50 oxen carcasses when his party reached the next water source. He described the playa in September as looking like "a plain of ice" and "a long lagoon of light blue water," a mirage so realistic in appearance that "oxen had stampeded for it, hoping to quench their burning thirst, and left their swelled up carcasses over the plain in that direction, as far as we could discern them."

The first picture we have of the Black Rock playa was made during the 1854 survey of the 38th parallel, which sought a central transcontinental railroad route across the West. The expedition artist, Prussian-born Friedrich W. von Egloffstein, made four topographical panoramas of the journey, starting from the Great Salt Lake Desert, crossing Nevada, and ending in northern California. The third in the series, *Valley of the Mud Lakes,* covers more than 80 miles east to west of the Black Rock playa and what is sometimes defined as its large southwestern lobe, the Smoke Creek Desert. The scene is so desolate that, were it not for the diminutive presence of the survey's leader and his horse in the foreground, plus a few birds in the sky, our eye would have nothing to prevent it from simply rolling around the playa like a loose marble. The "mud lakes" were the Black Rock and Smoke Creek playas, flooded when the artist saw them, hardly a typical condition.

The master cartographer of the ancient Lake Lahontan was Israel C. Russell, a young geologist who came to Nevada to trace its shore in 1881 and in his first field season covered 3,500 miles solo on horseback. It is with Russell that we have the first poet of the Black Rock. In his 1885 report, *Geological History of Lake Lahontan: A Quaternary Lake of Northwestern Nevada,* Russell echoed Frémont by saying that we must compare the Great Basin to the deserts of Arabia and to the shores of the Dead Sea. He wrote of the playas becoming "so sun-cracked as to resemble tessellated pavements of cream-colored marble" and described the Black Rock at midday: "When the sun is high in the cloudless heavens and one is far out on the desert at a distance from rocks and trees, there is a lack of shadow and an absence of relief in the landscape that make the distance deceptive—the mountains appearing near at hand instead of leagues away—and cause one to fancy that there is no single source of light, but that the distant ranges and the desert surfaces are self-luminous."

This is a description that fits the more usual condition of the playa and how it appeared to us this afternoon when we first broached the visual boundary of the Black Rock Desert. Russell also gave us a clue as to how facts can only circle around the nature of the desert, and that to approach its heart we must also deploy imagery and metaphor. As a species, we are mentally so unprepared for the playa that we cannot see it for what it is. Without the visual benchmarks of the mixed woodlands and savanna landscapes in which we evolved as hominids—without trees to show us our scale in the landscape and without humidity to fade the mountains with distance—we are lost. We have no ingrained mental templates to help us gauge how large or small we are in the space we occupy, how far it is to water or even to the next person. What looks like a car a mile away turns out to be a tin can resting on its side. What looks like an hour's walk is more than a day off. Light comes from every angle.

Such cognitive dissonance can kill you, or it can be used to your advantage. People die on the Black Rock every year because they misjudge its size and scale and their place within it. But it is also where the fifth-largest city in the state is created for a week prior to Labor Day weekend, when more than 25,000 people gather to celebrate the Burning Man Festival. The absolute absence of familiar surroundings, the lack of earthly constraints, allows for and encourages people to experience the planet in a profoundly different manner. Some people temporarily lose their social restraints during the gathering, while others make up fresh rules; marriages fall apart, but new relationships form; people change their mind, their career, their religion during Burning Man, and it's mostly the result not of artificial chemical alterations but of the under-appreciated yet overwhelming influence upon them of a geography so extreme they're knocked out of customary notions of space and time.

To apprehend, then, both the appearance and meaning of the Black Rock Desert, you have to camp in the middle of the playa. You learn to deal with the cognitive dissonance by using both cartographic and poetic tools. When I was here two weeks ago during Burning Man, a plastic orange mesh fence sur-rounded five square miles. Inside was a city with streets, a com-plete civic infrastructure, and more pyrotechnics lighting up the night sky than Fourth of July at Disneyland. Now the playa has returned to its constituent elements of light and air, a tabula rasa that has been erased clean. It is ready for our consideration, and we will find out if we are ready for its.

It's early evening as we make our first camp with Alvin, 110 miles out of Reno. Turning onto a dirt road at the base of the Granite Mountains, we drove first to a spot that Alvin and I have camped at before, up in the cottonwoods next to a creek. It had been fenced off recently, however, by a corporation none of us have ever heard of. And so we retreated back to a battered campsite closer to the playa, happy to find at least one spot still acces-sible.

The remnants of a calf rot in the sagebrush a few yards away, and although the flies are numerous, the decomposition is so advanced that there's no smell. Presumably the livestock here belongs to the corporation, but if this is evidence of their management style, they're going to have to learn a few things about the complicated coexistence of ranching and recreation on the edge of a desert where everything is open to intense inspection by visitors.

detritus

On his knees, with his head upside down in order to peer through the ground glass of his 4 x 5 large-format camera, which is usually positioned on the top of the tripod head but at this moment is screwed onto the bottom, Mark is lining up a broken beer bottle, a shell casing, and my figure walking in from the horizon. It's our first morning working out on the desert, and we've stopped mid-playa while on our way to Black Rock Springs, which sit at the foot of Black Rock Point.

Playas resurface themselves every winter, rain melting the silt and smoothing out the surface, and huge, thin sheets of ice pushed around by the wind polishing the mud until it shines.

What's left behind by humans takes a surprisingly long time to sink underground and also reemerges periodically as the sediments are churned by weather. The forefinger-sized .50-caliber cannon shell, which Mark spotted from our moving vehicle, dates from the late 1940s, a post–World War II artifact that recently crossed over the fifty-year-old threshold into official status as a protected historical resource. Honoring this, we picked it up, examined the mottled green verdigris on the brass, then put it carefully back into the shallow depression into which it will eventually subside.

The military has an affinity for playas, starting with mapping them by the Army Corps of Topographical Engineers and extending through using them as gunnery ranges during the war and as staging areas today for antiterrorist exercises. The Black Rock hasn't been an active target for decades—though overflights by fighters and occasional troop drops still occur near where we're parked—but the evidence of its strategic position is all around us. Lightweight targets were towed behind planes during World War II, and fighter pilots practiced shooting them down with bursts of machine gun fire. The targets have disappeared, but the ejected shells and their rusty brackets are scattered all over this northern end of the playa.

There are larger, 20mm shells as well. The slugs are harder to find, though we do see one or two decomposing into the silt. In addition to the spent shells, a live .50-caliber round rests nearby, probably ejected at the end of a belt to clear the breech. It is most likely a dud by now, but people are still maimed by World War II munitions that they pick up out in the deserts of the American West, so we leave it alone.

Bullet casings found on the playa

The juxtaposition of the shell next to the amber-colored beer bottle that Mark is photographing makes manifest the story of how the desert in general, and the playas in particular, have evolved from their status as a military asset to a recreational one. Starting in the late 1950s, the pace of visitation to the Black Rock began to pick up as the American economy came out from under the shadow of the war, Jeeps became available to the venturesome, and the population of the West began to boom again. Over the next three days we will find extensive evidence of the change, including shells from nine different caliber weapons, from old 20mm shells more than twice the size of my thumb to brand-new civilian 9mm pistol and petite .22 rifle shells. Along with the inevitable beer bottles, aluminum cans, and plastic soft drink containers, we'll stumble onto the lower jaw of a coyote, a moccasin, innumerable scraps of lumber, scorched hobby rocket launch pads, golf tees, and a light scattering of prehistoric lithic flakes.

The Black Rock has been a place for people to scavenge ever since the immigrants passed through, abandoning all manner of implements and household goods as they fought to get across the playa lest they, too, come to rest on its surface. Most of their artifacts have long since been scooped up by visitors, along with every piece of flaked stone larger than a dime, evidence of the human habitation that's been in the larger Black Rock Desert for at least 9,000 years. Amateur artifact hunting throughout the area has limited the opportunities for professional archeologists, anthropologists, and historians to recover the past, as it has over much of the West, which is one of the reasons there is now an Antiquities Act protecting such items.

Lithic sherds and metal fragments, artifacts from Hardin City

The golf tees take some explaining. "Lucifer's Anvil" is lettered on their sides, the name of the course set out annually by Doug Keister, a photographer from the Bay area, and his friends. Keister is a nongolfer, which is exactly why he chose the playa in 1988 as a place to hold a tournament, there being no traditional hazards on what would be the world's largest fairway. People come from as far away as Australia to play nine more or less permanent holes comprising the course and use bicycles to retrieve the orange balls that they quite sensibly use. Putts of 150 feet are common.

All this is not to suggest that the Black Rock is littered with traces of activity, human or otherwise. Despite hosting an estimated 50,000 people a year, half of whom come for Burning Man, the vast majority of its surface is clear of all evidence, except for the thousands of temporary vehicle tracks that will disappear in a few months with the advent of winter.

Mark concentrates on the beer bottle, getting the foreground into close focus, then changes places with me so I can photograph his out-of-focus figure as it emerges from the distance. At first he's such an indistinct shape that he's more like a walking shadow than a figure, an odd reversal of figure to ground, as if the subject matter of a painting had changed places with the canvas. The camera is upside down, the picture on the ground glass is upside down, and the ground is brighter than the sky. It's a conspiracy of visual elements so severe that cognition is suspended momentarily. You could believe anything.

Bottle neck from the 1930s, the Black Rock playa

speed

Alvin McLane has been driving on the Black Rock Desert since 1958, the year he moved out to Reno from West Virginia. I'm fond of saying that he's covered more of Nevada on foot than any other man in the history of the state, and I'm pretty sure it's true, if unprovable. But for all the climbing over, caving under, and just plain hiking through its terrain at a breakneck pace, he's not been averse to driving a variety of four-wheel-drive vehicles anywhere they can go without unnecessarily disturbing the land. That is to say, he doesn't like leaving new tire prints on the ground. Even on the playa, which each year has so many tire tracks drawn on it that it looks like it's been furrowed acre by acre, he tries to stay in the shallow ruts that define the three main seasonal roads that cross the flats, one each branching from outside Gerlach straight to the Black Rock Range, up the west arm to Soldier Meadows, and into the east arm. This does not, however, make it any easier to follow the man.

I'm dogging Alvin's metallic blue Jeep in the minivan, repeatedly crossing his tracks in order to avoid at least some of the alkali dust that nonetheless gets so thick in the rented vehicle that it's difficult to breathe. He's hustling along at 65 miles per hour, the normal speed out here for local ranchers using the playa as the shortest and least disruptive route from one end of the desert to another. There's a county-maintained dirt road that runs roughly parallel to us south of the playa, elevated up onto the alluvial soils on the other side of the railroad tracks, but its washboarding is legendary to drivers in three states, and we all avoid it as much as possible. Besides, speeding along without any posted limits, hell, without any enforced road, is exhilarating. I'm closing in on 80 as I try to get out from under the dust cloud Alvin's kicking up.

Speed here kills, though, as surely as on an L.A. freeway, and Mark and I were stopped earlier in the day by the Gerlach Search and Rescue truck, its lights flashing, the driver waving us down. "Have you guys seen any motorcycles? We have a report of one down out here somewhere."

We were appalled, unable to imagine trying to locate something as small as a motorcycle lying on its side in the middle of the flat. We hadn't seen any bikes since early morning, when what looked to be a pair of two café racers floated across the

"S" curve made by a vehicle crossing desiccation cracks

middle of the basin, their drivers thrust down almost double, chins to the short handlebars designed for hyperfast bikes. Later we found out that the front wheel of a bike had clipped the rear tire of the leader, flipping one rider into death and the other into intensive care.

Alvin has zipped up and down the playa for years, a careful if fast driver, though one curiously willing to plow headlong at high speed in an open Jeep into one of the frequent afternoon dust storms that are so thick they turn broad daylight into the sort of dim gloom-and-doom atmosphere the movies would have us believe resides in ancient Egyptian tombs. A picture of him taken afterward shows a sunburned visage whited out by alkali, his hair standing out straight behind him. My first experience of the playa at high speed occurred in 1992 while coming out to an early episode of Burning Man. Started on a beach in San Francisco in 1986, the festival had grown so large in three years that the police closed it down and founder Larry Harvey moved it to the Black Rock. In 1992, the second year the event was held in Nevada, six hundred of us showed up, having been given directions that told us only to drive ten minutes out onto the playa, then turn left and go until we saw people.

Following these instructions, my girlfriend and I found ourselves blasting alongside several other vehicles, all of us going over 60 and leaving behind a long curtain of thick alkali that hung in the air without dispersing for several minutes. The dry lakebed rolled underneath the front of the car as if the land were moving, not us. It was dizzying, disorienting, exciting, and vaguely terrifying. You had the sense that everything would be fine unless it wasn't, and you couldn't do anything about it either way, the sort of inevitability you feel when riding in a speedboat very fast over large ocean waves with someone else steering. You can get seasick in either instance, your mind unable to correlate the motion correctly with what your eyes are seeing and your body is sensing, which on the playa is almost nothing. An occasional light bump marks the crossing of a rut made by another vehicle, perhaps when the playa was damp; otherwise, it's a very smooth ride, which is exactly why efforts to break the land speed record moved here from the Bonneville Salt Flats in 1985.

People from southern California still drag their souped-up cars, trucks, motorcycles, and even modified RVs to the flats east of Wendover, Utah, seeking to break one record or another. But not only does the salt have to be planed flat each spring after the winter waters recede, leaving behind a surface severely dished by pressure ridges, but the thickness of the salt itself has been steadily declining from groundwater pumping by a nearby mining operation. The serious contenders have moved operations to the Black Rock, which requires little more preparation than marking out a straight line. In 1997 Andy Green, a former RAF jet jockey, became the first person to break the sound barrier in a car on land when he reached 763 mph in the 54-foot-long, twin-jet-engine Thrust SSC. Alvin and I watched one of the runs from outside Gerlach, the desert at one second featureless, at the next a 10-mile-long wall of alkali hanging in the air above where the supersonic car had run.

Playas invite blind speed, and an artist I know who grew up

in western Nevada used to go out at night to a microplaya near Yerington to play car tag with his friends in the moonlight, driving after each other with their lights off. Then there's that climactic scene from the movie *The Misfits,* the last film made by Clark Gable and Marilyn Monroe, both of them dead soon after. Riding out on the playa in a pickup to chase wild horses, lassoing them with ropes tied to old tires as draglines, they rocked and rolled across the alkali until Monroe, even on black-and-white film, was palpably green around the gills.

Today, however, I have a different problem while following Alvin. Weaving in and out of his dust cloud, I've settled for a speed of about *75* mph on a faint track just parallel to the deeper one he's using, but I'm having trouble paying attention to what I'm doing. There's nothing to focus on, his Jeep invisible, the playa uniformly tracked in all its flat directions. My mind wanders. It's a shock when I bounce across a small mound, then another and another. The minivan rattles ominously. The bumps rise only a few inches or so above the surface, but to a smaller vehicle, say, a motorcycle, at this speed they could be deadly.

I pass through the mounds in seconds, radically reconfiguring the front-end alignment before I really have any time to react— not that violent maneuvers would be advisable in any case— and guide the van back into Alvin's dust. The steering wheel now requires some force to keep me from drifting right, which actually helps me maintain attention.

Soon enough we're approaching the Black Rock itself, the dark stony mass that sits at the junction of the east and west arms of the desert. It has taken us forty-five minutes to cross what was once a multiday death march that immigrants faced in the late 1840s. Back then it was lack of speed that was deadly, a race with heat, distance, dehydration, exhaustion.

The Black Rock Desert is surrounded by mountains uplifted on faults, the playa sitting in a basin formed by a down-dropped block, which in turn is covered with alluvial debris carried down from the mountains. The playa is the terminus for runoff from approximately 2,600 square miles, and the sediments are more than a mile thick in places, beds of clay and gravel, minerals and salts having accumulated for millions of years.

Along the base of the mountains on the south side of the playa is a fault dotted with geothermal springs; the fault trends northeastward from the mountains to Black Rock, where a clear pool averaging 133.25° F bubbles in a grass-lined bowl of tufa, or calcium carbonate. A cutoff of the immigrant trail passes by the spring on its way north and up the west arm of the desert toward Oregon, and it's near here where we'll camp, at the foot of the landmark.

Alvin continues to lead the way, following a road that now weaves among the phreatophyte mounds that mark the edge of the playa as the land begins to rise slightly. Unlike the low mounds I've just driven over, these four- to six-foot-high ones are caused by vegetation, salt-tolerant plants that send roots down to live on subsurface water. As the winds blow, sand accumulates around the base of the plants, forcing them to grow higher. A mound starts to form under the plant, lifting it upward a few inches year by year until it is several feet high and the roots can no longer reach the water. The plant dies, the mound slowly erodes, and the sand is free to blow once more under a new plant. It is a fragile, slow cycle, one of many manifestations of time visible to the naked eye in the desert.

panorama

Mark has scrambled up the side of the Black Rock, a precipitous and crumbling mass of sedimentary and volcanic fragments, and selected a vantage point from which to make sweep-
ing views of the playa. In the afternoon light he can only guess
what the basin will look like the next morning, but he has a
good idea of where the sun will rise, how the long shadows of
the Black Rock Range will add texture to the desert floor, and
how the far mountains will provide a wall from which vision
can bounce back toward the viewer, thus providing, if not scale,
at least a horizon line to contain the picture. Alvin and I loll
around in our camp below, watching him pick his way deli-

cately around the scree, which is balanced right at the angle of repose and therefore inclined to slide.

Here's the thing. The human eye collects light and the brain sees. Or, more correctly, the eye is actually part of the brain, a neurological scanner that collects light reflected from around the landscape (or from photographs and paintings, for that matter) in a series of never-ending saccades, brief sweeps back and forth that seek boundary contrasts between light and dark, straight and not straight, inside and outside, and so on. The brain ignores most of the light it receives, organizing the view around approximately twenty-four basic shapes out of which it can construct a mental image of any landscape or other thing that's been scanned.

Now, what is the eye to do in an isotropic landscape where there's a uniform distribution of only a very few features . . . in fact, where the features themselves are roughly the same size and have the same number of sides, all so randomly different they're virtually identical? And where strong, unfiltered sunlight on a bright ground bleaches out most contrast?

This is what the playa is and what the unsorted polygons formed by its desiccation cracks are at midday. Its surface at a large scale is so uniform that your vision simply rolls around it; at your feet, at the scale of your body, it's so random that your brain can't keep hold of it—a severe problem for a photographer who's trying to pin its entirety on sheets of paper with a single large sweep.

A painter can manipulate the appearance and our perception of the playa by erasing the cracks and framing the valley with mountains, as Maynard Dixon did early in the twentieth century; a cinematographer can set wild horses to run a diagonal across it, as John Huston did on another Nevada playa when he filmed Monroe and Gable in *The Misfits*. But a still photographer has few choices.

It's no accident that the first overall visual record of a playa in North America may have been a panorama, the one drawn by von Egloffstein on the 1854 railroad survey, which was the basis for a lithograph in the published report. The accuracy of his artwork is verified by the original cartography done by Preuss when he passed through with Frémont.

Panoramas have an honorable place in the history of exploration, starting with coastal profiles sketched by Dutch and British sailors in the seventeenth century. Drawn from the decks of ships as they cruised new shores, the panoramas enabled explorers to map the contours of land from northern Europe to South America. The panoramic documentation of new landscapes continues today with the photographs made by Apollo astronauts on the moon using chest-mounted cameras.

As accurate a topographical view as could be obtained prior to the deployment of photography, the panoramic drawing was used to delineate the significant features of a landscape necessary for future navigation, and von Egloffstein's view of the Black Rock is no exception. *Valley of the Mud Lakes* is a view that covers roughly 7,200 square miles of topography. Reading from right to left, it shows the immigrant route from the Humboldt River drainage to the Black Rock Range, follows the playa as it stretches westward underneath the Granite Range, where we camped the first night, and then comes to the future site of Gerlach on the left. The mountains in the far background are more than 90 miles distant, across the border in what is now Oregon.

The Prussian did the best he could with the featureless playa by moving his vantage point back far enough to frame it with the surrounding mountains, then placing a figure in the foreground with his horse and dynamically arranging clouds and birds in the sky to push the viewer's attention downward onto the land. Mark does not have the option of dropping in clouds and birds, but in climbing up Black Rock Point he will follow the earlier artist's lead by including dark rocks and hills in the foreground. Our campsite will substitute for the rider and his horse, lending some human scale to both time and space.

Going to sleep that evening, our vehicles and tents splayed out not far from where the immigrant trail goes by the nearby hot spring, we watch the glow of moonrise brighten the mountain behind us. The sky is cloudless, the air still, the playa a silent, ghostly plain.

Mark is up before either Alvin or I, already situated on the ridge with his 4 x 5 camera mounted on its tripod well before daybreak. The morning light, when it comes, spreads swiftly across the playa, and he has only a few minutes to work while the shadows provide any kind of visual contrast with the flats. When done with the series of multiple shots he'll use to assemble a panoramic triptych, he moves the camera back to a new spot, sets the self-timer, and runs to the top of the vantage point from which he made the panorama.

Sunrise on the playa

Depicting Mark standing with his hands at his sides, the immigrant trail visible below him, it's a classic Klett photo, showing the viewer where the lens of the camera, and hence the mind of the photographer, was placed. It's a view that frames the view that frames the view. He's saying to us that the construction of landscape is an endless set of regressing mirrors, that there's always a larger context, and that each one is assembled by a person with a mental as well as physical point of view. We can't get outside the artist's frame when viewing the photograph, any more than we can climb outside words to discuss language. The panoramic view made from an elevated place can be an accurate tool, but it's no more privileged or objective than any other view, despite its larger frame of inclusion.

Seeing Mark photograph himself so that the viewer will see and then can set aside awareness of the artist in the body of work—making it a matter of conscious choice versus automatic assumption—reminds me of how we organize geographical facts about the Black Rock as if they were developed independent of human means. But even scientific facts are framed within terms chosen by individuals and adopted consensually, whether it's the notoriously and eccentrically defined length of a mile or the assignment of numerical values to scenic worth by government agencies. It's not that the terms are arbitrary or so relative as to be meaningless; far from it. But juxtaposing art with the science lets us step back to a larger frame, a more panoramic understanding of our perceptual mechanisms, than would be afforded by looking through the lens of a single discipline.

The virtue of any large and relatively empty space, whether

desert or ocean or ice cap, is that all of these considerations are both more visible and more comprehensible. We can't help but question how our perceptions work because they are freed from distraction, in a sense having nothing else to do. Isotropic spaces provide us with so little to process from the exterior environment that we tend to focus on the interior, which may be one reason why the world's monotheisms are traditionally considered to have arisen in the desert.

The photographic landscape panorama is an art object, a cartographic aid, and a scientific tool that is well suited to the Black Rock. It's one of the few ways to capture a sense of the playa's size and uniformity, and it provides a visual correlate to its maps while also documenting its natural and human status in a specific time. It's also the logical and aesthetic counterpoint to suspending the camera a few inches off the ground to picture the intricacies of a desiccation fissure, a jawbone, a bullet. Between the two kinds of photographs, the panoramic and the closeup, Mark is beginning to bracket our experience of the playa.

surface

Taking a Brunton pocket transit out of his pack—essentially an augmented compass—Mark walks off into some thin brush on the northern end of the playa, turns around, and motions me to walk slowly backward up a low berm. In my right hand I hold a long and straight branch that we found on the ground, nothing that grew on the playa but one that must have washed down from the mountains. The object of his attention is the singularly abrupt elevation change in this part of the desert.

The playa where we're working is runneled with erosion channels carved several feet deep in the solidified gray dust, and I'm standing on the outermost point of an old spit left over from when a 500-foot-deep lake once stood here, a relict body of water from the Pleistocene that last receded 6,000 years ago. This is what's left of its shoreline. On the mountains around us, we can trace dozens of terraces that are the remnants of ancient beaches. *Playa,* in Spanish, means beach, and despite the chronic lack of water in the Black Rock during the course of human history, it's a perfectly appropriate word.

Mark, although standing only a few yards from me, is positioned in the Quinn River Sink, that low point of the Black Rock playa where the river, which flows in wet years out of the 9,000-foot Jackson Mountains to the northeast, finally debouches. Maps label this an area to avoid because its surface conditions are unpredictable; the clay can remain wet just beneath a deceptively dry crust even in the summer. This has been unfortunate for some. Four-wheel-drive vehicles stuck out here, nearly 30 miles north of Gerlach and the nearest tow truck, must be left in place until the ground dries out before they can be retrieved, which can take weeks or months. People have been known to walk away from their truck stuck in a playa and just buy a new one.

Mark measures the relief from the sink to the top of the shoreline, where we're parked, at six and a half feet. As he walks from his spot to mine, he crosses a single type of soil that varies from being so delicately cracked that it resembles layers of gold foil to forming a hardpan that admits no impression of his sandals.

As flat as the playa is, displaying only five feet of elevation change over a 25-mile stretch, what is underfoot nonetheless changes constantly. On the Wednesday of my arrival at Burning

Man two weeks ago, the finely fractured surface of the playa resembled nothing so much as a jigsaw puzzle fit together with impossible precision. For all intents and human purposes, the irregular and unsorted polygons created by desiccation fissures were infinite in all directions. Trying to count them within the nearest six square feet was impossible and made me dizzy.

Thursday morning it rained lightly, the clays of the playa swelling, the cracks disappearing. The playa had become a monolithic plain as far as one could see—as if it were the uncomplicated ground of a virtual reality game—for all of an hour before the cracks reappeared, the very same ones. Their underlying structure in the clay can extend underground for several feet and thus persevere through rainstorms. The physics of how the fissures form and maintain coherence has yet to be fully explained, though it seems likely to be rooted in geometrical crystalline structures at the molecular level and is thus a deeply rooted persistency.

Friday night it poured. Walking the two miles back to my tent from the midnight burning of a sculpture—an elaborately constructed two-story wooden temple—took almost an hour. Every few steps my shoes acquired three inches of dense mud, which would then fall off one shoe or the other, leaving me to walk lopsided the entire time. People were carrying their bicycles over one shoulder, an otherwise excellent form of transportation for the playa immobilized by mud packed up to the fenders.

The next day the playa cracked anew, the edges of the polygons upturned like crisp earthen leaves. Our 50,000 bare feet, shoes, boots, and sandals ground them into a fine alkali flour that blew about in the daily afternoon wind and in turn accumulated into small fugitive dunes around every tent peg, food box, automobile tire, or other temporarily immobile object.

The local people who land-sail out here on their elongated, low-slung, three-wheeled craft have submitted a formal complaint to the Bureau of Land Management (BLM), which is responsible for issuing permits to the Burning Man organization. They want to force a full environmental impact study of the event, the primary basis of their complaint being that it has grown too large and that the fugitive dust caused by so many people has collected in small dunes they call "playa snakes." They find these dangerous to their health when flying over the desert at 50 mph on their dirt boats.

They're right about one thing: the dunes are a hazard. These small irregularities are what I encountered in the rental van our first day out, and I would not want to hit them at high speed while sailing along a few inches off the alkali. But no one has established any cause and effect yet, and the BLM is monitoring the dunes, which could as easily have been caused by supersonic cars racing in the same area of the desert, by casual day users on off-road vehicles, or by unknown subsurface dynamics of the playa. Such dunes, in fact, have formed out here before, most notably in the early 1970s, well before these user groups were present in any numbers. Some scientists speculate that they may result from the Quinn River flash-flooding the playa during severe conditions, another possibility that is being monitored by the BLM.

The flatness of the playa is its greatest virtue. The uniformity creates a unique viewshed, as well as the supreme ground upon which to test the speed of our imagination. Although the playa is furrowed in every direction over most of its extent by drivers exercising the utter freedom to venture where they will without lines, lights, curbs, or signs, almost every mark will be erased in a normal winter. Rain will fill in the cracks and tracks, and wind will push around thin sheets of water, 10 by 40 miles in extent, that will polish the basin floor. Freeze-and-thaw cycles will puff up the surface into soft clumps that the wind and water will again break down into mud, then dust, further erasing our passage.

We take the playa to be a perpetually blank slate, a tabula rasa, which in Latin means a tablet that is scraped clean. Aristotle used the Greek equivalent in the fourth century B.C. to describe the human mind at birth, an idea resurrected in 1690 by the English philosopher John Locke, who compared the mind to a white sheet of paper awaiting the inscription of experience. Out on the playa, in the midst of a landscape we imagine to be perfectly blank, we await novel experiences that will reveal something of the world to us that we haven't seen before.

The locals who want to keep large events off the Black Rock are not, perhaps, arguing so much against people being out there as they are attempting to keep the slate clean. After surveying the elevation changes on the northern end of the playa, Mark and I drive down toward its middle, following coordinates furnished by the Burning Man organizers for the main burn site from two weeks earlier. The navigational numbers are displayed on his handheld global positioning system unit, and once we're out of the Quinn River Sink and the playa resumes its customary level state, Mark doesn't even look at the ground while driving, keeping his eyes on the GPS unit and steering according to the arrows on its screen.

Once we reach the site, we get out and walk in widening circles to find traces of the event. Off to our east the forty-person cleanup crew that's picking up after the event is walking a grid over every square inch of the five square miles in what was recently Black Rock City. They haven't gotten here yet, but even so, we find only a single pink boa feather and no significant remains. A small pile of fugitive dust is marked by an orange traffic cone and will be broken up, dispersed, and then watered down in order to reintegrate it with the surface.

Burning Man, too, depends on the blankness of the Black Rock, the very quality that fires up the imagination of its participants. It's in their aesthetic and philosophical interests to clean the slate, as well as a matter of honoring their contract with the BLM, which will send out personnel in two more weeks to sample silt both on and off site, comparing levels of contamination in randomly selected transects. Everyone has a vested interest in the surface.

Mark's biggest fear about the changing "nature" of people in the outdoors has to do with the organized mediation of our experiences. Government agencies in control of public lands, faced with the pressures of a rapidly increasing population, tend to channel people onto paved roads that lead only to designated

Abandoned house, now historic site, at the edge of the playa

campgrounds, thus preserving the rest of the landscape from not only damage but in some cases even traces of passage. This has led to more and more land, especially in the West, being closed off to vehicular traffic and sometimes even to people on foot. Mark notes that this paternalistic attitude breeds resentment toward the restrictions, causing more and more people to violate them, and argues that widespread education is the answer. Don't remove the ability of people to explore the world for themselves, he contends, but teach them how to do it responsibly.

The BLM has recently proposed a new management plan for the Black Rock that would institute fees to be used to build and maintain an interpretive center and a primitive campground. This, too, is something neither Mark and I nor the nearby residents are eager to see. The BLM wants urgently to preserve the viewsheds into and across the playa; the rangers from the Winnemucca field office clearly recognize the value of its blankness, a rather unique scenic resource compared to the more stereotypically sublime climaxes of Yosemite and the Grand Canyon.

Nowhere else are these conflicting ideas about landscape, and our commitment to rediscovery in it, more evident than on the surface of the playa, a landscape that remakes itself each year, an analog for the tabula rasa of wilderness, the world at birth.

mirage

Later in the day Mark is driving us back toward the Black Rock and our last campsite, steering by the GPS, again holding the unit in his hand on the dashboard. His eyes are on the small screen, not the ground, and he steers by lining up a directional arrow with the electronic graphic of a road. But there is no road in front of us. We both look at the screen, ignoring the outside for minutes at a time. At 60 miles an hour, it will be at least a quarter of an hour before we have to pay attention to what's outside the vehicle. This driving style is getting to be a habit.

To work, the GPS unit needs to read signals from at least four satellites in order to triangulate our position, and the more

Driving by the GPS, approaching the Black Rock from the west, 5.58 miles

fixes it can establish, the more accurate it can plot us. On the playa there is nothing in the path of the signals, and we're reading five of them. This is a large improvement over the existing maps from the United States Geological Survey, the agency that eventually was created by Congress to take over the duties of the U.S. Army Corps of Topographical Engineers.

The USGS maps, based on aerial surveys with ground controls, show most of the Black Rock as blank white paper, a corner occasionally crossed by a single contour line indicating a foot or two of elevation up or down, a slope that is imprecise to begin with and subject to change each year as silts are redistributed by runoff. On some of the maps even the national grid fails. Whereas solid lines on most maps organize almost all of America into township squares, on some topographical maps the grid on the Black Rock is indicated only by dotted lines, meaning that there never was any ground control, no fixed point that was linked to the maps, definitively confirming latitude and longitude. And now that there's the GPS, the agency might not ever bother; what would be the purpose? The great playa remains, for all intents, unmapped.

Earlier in the day, when we piloted ourselves to the coordinates where the Burning Man was torched two weeks ago, we couldn't have found the site of the burning without the GPS and numbers furnished by the organization. The BLM was out here last week attempting to find where David Best had torched the two-story wooden temple he'd erected, and even with the coordinates they couldn't find the burn spot. But, then, David had literally vacuumed his site afterward. All that exists from the event are memories and pictures.

After we finished walking the site, we continued driving south toward Gerlach, stopping when we spotted a mirage out ahead of us by two or three miles, which is typically the distance at which this optical phenomenon is observed. Formed by the abrupt boundary between air masses of two temperatures, mirages are frequent on the playa, where the air immediately above the ground is much hotter than just a few inches higher. The subsequent discontinuity causes light to bend, or refract, the most common effect being to reflect back the sky, an illusion that today was a blue line that thickened until it resembled a vast lake in front of us that stretched across the entire width of the playa. This was the kind of mirage Bruff wrote about, livestock crazed with thirst stampeding themselves to death for an optical apparition.

Mark hauled out the large-format camera and had me hold up one of the tubes of my binoculars to the lens. He focused on the magnified image of the mirage through both camera and what had become, in essence, a small telescope, and we waited.

Within minutes a shape began to precipitate out of the illusion, a dark and indistinct figure that was akin to how Mark had appeared two days ago while walking in toward the beer bottle for the photograph. If, in either case, you didn't know beforehand what you were looking at, you couldn't tell what was headed your way. We had no idea. Objects on the playa that stick up above the mirage layer are seen as doubled—the light reflected from the top of the object comes straight at you through

View through Bill's binoculars: truck two miles distant approaching
through a mirage on the playa

the cooler air, while the light reflected from the bottom goes down into the hot air, then bounces back up to you. As a result, you see a doubled image, the top half right side up, the bottom upside down.

The shutter clicked. Mark removed the film, put in another film holder, and clicked again, shooting away until what turned out to be a pickup truck solidified out of the mirage. It was driven by ranchers headed up the west arm toward Soldier Meadows, who politely slowed down as they passed in order to avoid covering us with more than a light dusting of alkali, then sped up once they were by. Mark and I examined one of the Polaroid prints.

Almost always Mark leaves a trademark frame around his pictures, printing all the way out to the edge of the Polaroid negative, which shows the viewer a bit of the processing chemicals still on the edges. It's another way of reminding people that this is a photograph made by a person with a singular viewpoint, not an objective reality seen the same by all witnesses.

The mirage photo is instead framed by the round lens of the monocular optics, the truck doubled above and below the plane of the mirage, object and its reflection hovering in an indeterminate field of vision. The picture was blurry, crude, very nineteenth century, and showed how the playa is scored by parallel vehicle tracks, which ran away under the mirage.

More than any other photo of the Black Rock that I've ever seen, this one captured the difficulty we have of determining where we are out here, GPS or not. By being able to view a test Polaroid print minutes after making the photograph, we had directly experienced the mirage, then both documented and transformed it through layered optics into an art object, and now we had a visual record that would itself influence how we looked at the desert during our next and final day. In that sense the photo and my writing about it made a collaborative snapshot not just of how the mirage appeared but of how we frame perception itself.

The hardest thing to know is the mind, that aggregate of endlessly looping and self-reflexive processes that take place within the most complicated structure of which humankind is aware. Eighty percent of all information we take in is visual. The playa, by virtue of its relative blankness, affords us a unique opportunity to view the mind at work, as there is comparatively little to visually distract us. The other senses are likewise subdued by the lack of stimuli. The mind wanders, its neural extension, the eye, looking for contours, boundaries, and shapes it can sort into hazards to be avoided, resources to be exploited. Finding little to grasp, it turns to contemplate itself. If there were nothing else to recommend the preservation of the Black Rock, this cognitive viewshed alone would be worth saving.

Mark keeps steering toward the Black Rock, making minute adjustments of the steering wheel with the help of the GPS, then slides off to the right and southward, seeking a place to camp that's isolated from all three of the dirt tracks that cross the playa, somewhere the tire marks are less frequent. We end up back on the edge of the Quinn River Sink, the edge of the old shoreline just visible to the southeast. The crackled pavement of the desert shines in the late sun, light and heat coming at us from all directions.

sky

We pick our last campsite by letting the van roll to a stop in the middle of absolutely nothing in particular. This is unusual. Mark and I are used to driving until dark looking for the ideal place to set up a kitchen, some nook sheltered by trees and rocks. There's no point to that here, no point on the map to be selected over any other.

We make camp by placing the van between us and an intermittent breeze blowing from the east, spread out table and chairs, then wander about taking notes and photographs in the lengthening shadows. What we're here to do is observe the sky or, more precisely, watch how sky and ground interact in our vi-

Forty-foot shadows at camp number 3

sion, especially after having been more attuned to the issue by the mirage.

In some places in America the sky is very small, even though the land is large. If you stand on a clear day in a field in rural Oklahoma or Texas or Kansas, some place with not much visible relief to the ground, you will be able to see only 2.8 miles in any direction, and you will automatically limit the sky's circumference in your mind to match the radius of your sight. But where the ground is equally flat in all directions and mountains form the horizon 10 or 20 miles off, as can be the case on the Black Rock, and even though you do not see the level ground around you any farther than in the Midwest, your mind fills in the intervening space between you and the peaks. Suddenly the sky is enormous. Instead of experiencing 31 square miles on the ground, you apprehend 1,300 times that much. The sky, which before was a flat panel suspended over you as if a ceiling, assumes the vaulted stature of a planetary atmosphere. You understand what you are standing under, and it is visibly immense.

Many people claim you can see the curvature of the earth on the Black Rock, but that place of privilege exists nowhere on earth. The playa appears to swell in the middle, and the feet of the mountains are mostly invisible, as if dropping away over a spherical curve. It's the same phenomenon as when you see a ship sailing over the horizon: the hull disappears first, while the sails are still visible. But actually *see* the curvature? No. Scientists insist that you can't see the curvature of the planet from anywhere on its surface but must be at least 80,000 feet above it, as demonstrated by photographs taken repeatedly by astronauts.

In fact, the playa does curve, but the effect is local, not planetary, in nature, the result of its mile-deep clays and sediments soaking up water like an unfathomably large sponge. The playa rises in its center and drops down at its edges, where the water table rises close to the surface and the hardy plants reside atop their phreatophyte mounds, those humps of sand and dirt that even as they ascend are creating their own demise.

From the center of the playa, you can't see the mounds; they're too far away. You're still only seeing 31 out of the 400 square miles of surface, but the mountains force the illusion that you're seeing more. So, not only do you think you see the curvature of the earth, but now the sky performs a vault over your head. It appears to be a palpable dome, its edges curving downward to mate with the faraway ridge lines. It's another illusion, one that earthworks artist Jim Turrell has enhanced at Roden Crater in Arizona, having leveled the edges of the volcanic cinder cone so that, when you lie down in it on your back, the sky seems to deform itself down to meet the earth.

As the sun sets on the Black Rock, the shadows of the peaks during the last few seconds racing across the playa at up to 50 miles per hour, the vault deepens. To the east of our camp, the terminator, the shadow of the earth, rises above the horizon until it becomes so dark we can no longer see its progress. Mark and I slowly scan the entire horizon during the process, Mark taking slow exposures of what he says appears to be the largest

unbounded space he's ever been in. This is a remarkable statement, coming from a man who has spent the majority of his
adulthood in the largest and most open deserts of the American
Southwest and who, when younger, spent summers on the great
rolling and lonesome hills of Wyoming with the pocket transit,
tracing out likely coal deposits for the USGS.

But he's right. When it's completely dark, the camp stove
off, the dishes done, and the small pallid scorpions that come
out at night to grasp each other's forelegs and mate under our
feet have departed for their invisible burrows nearby, we turn
off our small lantern. The Milky Way arcs overhead like a bright
road to the back of the universe. We hold out our arms parallel
to its course and begin to revolve under it; within two rotations
the sky, too, has begun to spin. We risk three or four revolu-
tions, craning our heads back to spot a star, much as a ballet
dancer picks out and focuses on a spot on a wall to keep from
getting dizzy during pirouettes . . . but it's no use. We stop to
stagger about, slightly nauseated, the earth still reeling beneath
our feet. There's nothing in the darkness to focus on, to halt the
disorientation.

In a way, it's another kind of cognitive dissonance in the
desert, an example of how our minds fail to process accurately
what we are seeing—or in this case, not seeing. The most obvi-
ous example of such disorientation in daylight is our inability
to judge distance accurately out here. We're fooled both by the
lack of vertical elements such as trees or telephone poles, which
allow us to scale ourselves and the landscape, as well as mark it
off, and by the absence of atmospheric perspective, that blue

shift in the land's palette caused by humidity progressively scattering light the farther away from us it goes. By all rights the mountains should start to turn blue within a few miles, but they remain stubbornly brown, the air too dry to scatter the spectrum much and the vegetation too sparse even to assist the shift away from brown. We look at the mountains out around the Black Rock and think 5 miles instead of the actual 20 it is from here to there.

We're tricked also into a twilight zone of haptic confusion, where we're unable to form a sense of how our body connects to the space around it through any of our other senses. Apart from the smell of alkali dust, which our noses read perversely as damp cement sidewalks, there are no olfactory clues. Mark and I smell no flowers or pines or sagebrush, no diesel fumes or smog or chemicals. Even the food odors from our dinner disappeared quickly from air that is so dry it has trouble supporting molecules the nose can read.

And out here it's so quiet that the ringing in Mark's ears, which has plagued him gently ever since he can remember, becomes loud enough that it disturbs his concentration. Later in the night we'll no doubt hear the far-off rumble of freight trains that run along the southern rim of the playa, but for the moment there's nothing. No wind, no coyotes, no aircraft. We have the ground we stand on, the low mountainous silhouettes of the encircling horizon miles and miles away, and that intricate arc of the galaxy. We walk around in progressively larger circles, our heads back, eyes shut, for as long as we like without fear of bumping into anything, even each other.

Before going to bed we set up tents, not willing to share our sleeping bags with the small scorpions. Sitting in nylon folding chairs for a nightcap of blue agave tequila, we watch the moon rise through binoculars, a desert that has sailed over our heads each night we've been out on the Black Rock. It's just past full and shines through thin bands of clouds that hover improbably only in front of the moon, as if to give us a better show.

Mare Serenitatis, or the Sea of Serenity, the old name of the desolate lunar plains, echoes what we call the ocean when referring to its blank surface as "the desert of the sea." The open sea is the largest isotropic vista on the planet, but only from high above its surface—looking out from the bridge of a ship or looking down from an airplane or perhaps from a precipitous coastline—are we dimly aware of how large it is. "The sea of stars," we say, referring to the Milky Way. Beyond that is intergalactic space, the only infinite openness we can propose. Science fiction is littered with deserts that are the settings for imaginary dramas, from the early Martian novels of Edgar Rice Burroughs to the *Dune* series by Frank Herbert and the desert worlds of Hollywood. Just as arid lands offer us a chance to look inward, so they offer few visual realities with which to compete with the illusions of fiction.

Learning to navigate in the desert, to cope with and learn from the cognitive dislocations it offers, is apt preparation for astronauts and writers, and both take advantage of desert travel to train for their roles. The moon rises, appearing to shrink as it does, yet another illusion, this one fostered not by the bending

Moonrise over the Black Rock

of light rays, as is so often mistakenly thought, but by another mental template, one that is completely counterintuitive.

When low, the moon is near a horizon dotted with features that are familiar to us in size. Although we know the moon is far away, we see it so clearly that we think to ourselves it must be larger than it really is. Our mind inflates it to twice the size it will appear to be when high enough not to be forcibly compared with terrestrial features. Only when it rises, freeing itself from that visual juxtaposition, does it escape our intuition, receding into the small object it actually is, one floating in a wilderness so vast that we must fail to comprehend it.

. . . circumference

Once again Mark is up before sunrise, the camera positioned east of camp to freeze-frame the shadows that will stampede forth once the sun rises. When our elongated shadows do appear, they will move as we move yet show us where we are relative to the seasons and the time of day. Mark is forever photographing shadows, motioning those around him to come throw their dark projections into the field of view, contaminating what other artists would think a clean picture of the landscape. For him it's a way of including time within space.

For each campsite we pick, Mark prepares a stick game, which consists of a handmade shadow-casting assemblage of found

Stick game at sunrise

objects. First there's the stick, usually a piece of wood that Mark has carved and then adorned with symbolic mementos of the trip. Planting this marker in a clearing near camp, he then inscribes a circle several feet in diameter around it. Everyone places a token, also often fashioned from found materials, on its circumference. Whoever places the token closest to the shadow cast by the stick when the sun first hits it wins the game, having correctly predicted an intersection of space and time. Most often that's Mark. I credit his practice with shadows as the reason, not his sense of geodesy.

Last night in the dark after dinner, he finished the stick, a piece of greasewood found at our first camp in the trees and capped with the remnants of a bottle rocket. The stubby cardboard cylinder formed a cup to hold the tokens, various cartridge shells we've found on the playa. Rooting the stick after watching the moon rise, we line up the cartridges like metal seashells on a prehistoric beach. Much to our surprise this morning, it turns out we planted the game right at the intersection of two vehicle tracks.

The sun rises, blue shadows racing out from the mountains, Mark, the camera, and the stick. Almost immediately they begin to shorten into oblivion as the earth rotates to face the sun more directly. The shadows move fast enough to make you feel that you're standing on a body moving through space, experiencing a momentary vertigo that is as intensely satisfying as last night's spinning under the Milky Way. Both are specific sensations creating a connection to the planet as a whole, both almost impossible to feel among trees or buildings.

View from the tent, early morning

Before we break camp, Mark sets up tripod and camera in his tent, then lies down carefully underneath the rig to shoot a photograph. The picture will show his legs and feet resting in the open door of the tent, a triangle that frames the playa and distant hills. Like the juxtaposition of moon and horizon, this will fool the eye, making the playa look like an intimate back-yard that could be crossed on foot in an hour or two. Frames, I think, packing up the coffeepot; it's always about physical and mental frames.

We load up the van and drive off in a leisurely arc, prowling around the playa for most of the day, examining a linear field of phreatophyte mounds in the southern part of the playa that ex-isted when the immigrants came through, an important land-mark that has since been severely gnawed by all-terrain vehicles and motorcycles. This cultural erosion may do more than has-ten the natural process, and in ways we can't predict, subtly al-tering the interactions between groundwater and the surface of the desert. Golf tees litter the ground nearby, evidence of the periodic games played out on the world's longest and least en-cumbered fairways.

By midafternoon we're dusty enough to take a bath in Trego Springs, which sit on the fault running along the southern edge of the playa. The springs, too, are a kind of mirage, standing water in a pool next to the railroad track that was, indeed, placed along the route that von Egloffstein pictured in his panorama. Freight trains blow by at 70 mph, too fast for the engineer to do more than merely register the presence of a person.

We leave the playa late in the day, passing by the "stone boy"

Soaking in Trego Springs, south edge of the playa

"Stone boy" at the edge of the playa

that marks one of the three entrances onto the dry lake. Stacked rocks taller than a human, stone boys were traditionally erected by Basque sheepherders in the mountains above, monuments allowing them to establish sight lines in the large landscape. We don't know who built this one, which bears mute witness to traffic going onto and coming off the playa.

Parallel to the highway is Guru Road. Predating Burning Man by several years, it was at first the ongoing outsider art project of DeWayne Williams, a Gerlach resident who etched homilies on chunks of granite washed out of the mountains that rise north of the dirt road. We take our time traversing the installation, which over the years has been added to by many others. Some of the work celebrates anniversaries and memorializes the more laudable attributes of townsfolk; much of it is political, liberal, and antiestablishment slogans woven into antinuclear war sculptures. Crudely constructed but thoughtful parodies of weather stations, broadcasting booths, teepees, and wedding chapels are scattered amongst the sayings that line the road like miniature tombstones.

This linguistic assemblage has its origins equally in prehistoric rock art and in the huge whitewashed capital letters that schools erect on hillsides above their towns in the arid West, both messages proclaiming allegiance to locale. Not so much a direct commentary on the Black Rock, this collection yet exists precisely because of its blank backdrop. Wallace Stegner famously noted that we can't stand the deep silence of the arid West and are compelled to shout into its void. This is part of the shout.

So are the tracks left on the playa by cars, trucks, motor-

Installation artwork at Guru Road, edge of the playa

cycles, off-road vehicles, land sailors, and hikers, an intricate calligraphy traced in the alkali clay and silt, then erased by the seasonal recapitulation of the pluvial times that created the great lake covering most of the state, the terraced shorelines of which are all about us as we drive along the bordering mountains. Because the playa itself is not interrupted by the vertical elements we associate with time—buildings or trees, anything built or grown over an interval—we say it is a timeless landscape. Yet time is exactly what is visible here. Great spaces open up time to us; the more uniform the landscape, the more we are forced by our nature to perceive time.

The tracks come and go, the waters rise and recede, the sun pushes shadows around the playa like a herd of mops. The place is infinitely serious and wildly comic, encouraging the deepest kind of meditation and the exuberance of pyrotechnic festivals, giant golf games, and amateur rocket launchings.

Play, as a human activity, involves more neurons at a higher level of electrical excitation than any other activity, absorbs us even more than sex. Mark and I have been playing on the playa and, in doing so, paying it the most respect we know how.

Several weeks later we examine the photograph that Mark made of our first campsite before we drove out onto the playa. It's his habit, one more piece of the narrative frame in his ongoing collection of spaces turned into places by momentary habitation and memory. On the right side of the picture, our gear is scattered about, lit by the low sun that pours light across the dry lakebed and into the trees. But the negative of this first photo-

First camp on the playa (negative destroyed by heat)

graph has suffered extensive damage from heat after several days on the playa, and the left side is dark, a shadowy, almost black image of the tree under which we camped. Not only does the film record a space, but the image itself has been transformed by the place, a full circle of transformation that we also have undergone.

sources

The primary historical bibliographic resources for these meditations were four books:

John Charles Frémont, *A Report of the Exploring Expedition to the Rocky Mountains in the Year 1843, and to Oregon and North California in the Years 1843–44* (Washington, D.C.: U.S. Government Printing Office, 1845). The edition of this report that I use is the reprint edited by Donald Jackson and Mary Lee Spence, *The Expeditions of John Charles Frémont*, 2 vols. (Urbana-Champaign: University of Illinois Press, 1970). All quotes by Frémont are from volume 1.

Georgia Willis Reed and Ruth Gaines, eds., *Gold Rush: The Journals, Drawings, and Other Papers of J. Goldsborough Bruff, April 2, 1849– July 20, 1851* (New York: Columbia University Press, 1949).

Israel C. Russell, *Geological History of Lake Lahontan: A Quaternary*

Lake of Northwestern Nevada (Washington, D.C: United States Geological Survey, 1885). This the baseline book from which all other descriptions of the Great Basin geophysical region arise.

Sessions S. Wheeler, *Nevada's Black Rock Desert* (Caldwell, Idaho: Caxton Printers, 1978). Still the most popular text about the Black Rock, the book features several paintings by Craig Sheppard reproduced in black and white. Wheeler (1911–98) wrote several books about the Great Basin desert, including one on Pyramid Lake, all of which are informative sources.

During our foray onto the playa, the Bureau of Land Management, the federal agency responsible for stewardship of the Black Rock Desert, was soliciting comments on its new management planning document for the area, *Sonoma-Gerlach and Paradise Denio Management Framework Plan Amendment and Draft Environmental Impact Statement* (Winnemucca, Nevada: Winnemucca Field Office, Bureau of Land Management, August 2000). This is the most comprehensive single source of current and accurate information about the playa.

Information on the "playa serpents" was provided in personal communications from Mike Bilbo, in the Winnemucca Office. An informative handout by his wife, geomorphologist Barbara Bilbo, is *The Black Rock Desert Landscape* (Winnemucca, Nevada: Bureau of Land Management, 1999). It contains a short but excellent technical bibliography. In addition, the Bilbos directed me to two online sources of information: the USGS Ground Water Atlas at www.water.usgs.gov and the Texas Tech University playa site at www.lib.ttu.edu/playa.

William L. Fox's *The Void, the Grid, and the Sign* (Salt Lake City: University of Utah Press, 2000) investigates cognitive dissonance on the Black Rock, as well as its cartographic history. His *Playa Works: The Natural and Unnatural Histories of Dry Lakes* (Reno: University of Nevada Press, 2002), includes a chapter about Burning Man. A book by Fox and Mark Klett about the rephotographic work of Third View and the history of landscape photography in the West, *View Finder: Mark Klett, Photography, and the Reinvention of Landscape* (Albuquerque: University of New Mexico Press, 2001), investigates more thoroughly the notion of rediscovery in the land.

The panorama by von Egloffstein appears in Volume XI of the U.S. Congress publication *Reports of Exploration and Surveys to Ascertain the Most Practicable and Economical Route for a Railroad from the Mississippi River to the Pacific Ocean* (1861). Our thanks to Alvin McLane for letting us spend time with his copy.

about the author

William L. Fox has published fourteen collections of poetry, most recently *Reading Sand: Selected Desert Poems, 1976–2000*. His several nonfiction books investigate how we transform land into landscape through art, architecture, and memory. In 2002 he will participate in the National Science Foundation's Visiting Artists and Writers Program in the Antarctic and will be a visiting scholar at the Getty Research Institute and a Lannan Foundation writer-in-residence.

about the photographer

Mark Klett has been photographing the western landscape for more than twenty years. His publications include *Second View: The Rephotographic Survey Project, Revealing Territory, Traces of Eden,* and *Desert Legends* (with Gary Nabhan). He is the recipient of numerous awards, including three National Endowment for the Arts fellowships, a Japan–U.S. Friendship Commission fellowship, and the Buhl Foundation award. He is a Regents' Professor of Art at Arizona State University and the director of Third View, an ongoing project that revisits landscape photographs of the American West made during the 1860s and 1870s.

Library of Congress Cataloging-in-Publication Data

Fox, William L., 1949–

The Black Rock Desert / text by William L. Fox ; photographs by Mark Klett.

p. cm.— (Desert places)

Includes bibliographical references.

ISBN 0-8165-2172-7 (pbk. : alk. paper)

1. Black Rock Desert (Nev.)—Description and travel. 2. Black Rock Desert
(Nev.)—Pictorial works. 3. Black Rock Desert (Nev.)—History. 4. Natural
history—Nevada—Black Rock Desert. 5. Fox, William L., 1949– —Journeys—Nevada—Black Rock Desert. 6. Klett, Mark, 1952– —Journeys—
Nevada—Black Rock Desert. 1. Klett, Mark, 1952– 11. Title. 111. Series.

F847.B53 F69 2002

979.3'54—dc21

2001006275